Christian Evidence Series of b

EVIDENCE FOR GOD

by
Richard Swinburne
Professor of the Philosophy of Religion, University of Oxford

Published by Mowbray for
THE CHRISTIAN EVIDENCE SOCIETY

IN THIS SERIES:

Copyright © Richard Swinburne, 1986, 1988
ISBN 0 264 67124 4

First published 1986 for the Christian Evidence
Society by A.R. Mowbray & Co. Ltd., Saint Thomas
House, Becket Street, Oxford, OX1 1SJ.

Reprinted with amendments 1988

Typeset by Getset (BTS) Ltd., Eynsham, Oxford
Printed in Great Britain by Tisbury Printing Works Ltd., Salisbur

Evidence for God

WHY BELIEVE that there is a God at all? My answer is that to suppose that there is a God explains why there is a world at all; why there are the scientific laws there are; why animals and then human beings have evolved; why humans have the opportunity to mould their characters and those of their fellow humans for good or ill and to change the environment in which we live; why we have the well-authenticated account of Christ's life, death and resurrection; why throughout the centuries men have had the apparent experience of being in touch with and guided by God; and so much else. In fact, the hypothesis of the existence of God makes sense of the whole of our experience, and it does so better than any other explanation which can be put forward, and those are the grounds for believing it to be true. This short pamphlet seeks to justify this answer.

Each of the phenomena (things in need of explanation) which I have mentioned has formed the starting point of a philosophical argument for the existence of God, but all that philosophers have tried to do is to codify in a rigorous form the vague reasons which many ordinary men have had for believing that there is a God. These arguments seem to me to have a common pattern. Some phenomenon E, which we can all observe, is considered. It is claimed that E is puzzling, strange, not to be expected in the ordinary course of things; but that E is to be expected if there is a God; for God has the power to bring about E and he might well choose to do so.

Hence the occurence of E is reason for supposing that there is a God. E may be a large phenomenon, such as the existence of the Universe, or something a lot smaller, such as our own individual religious experiences.

The pattern of argument is one much used in science, history, and all other fields of human inquiry. A detective, for example, finds various clues – John's fingerprints on a burgled safe, John having a lot of money hidden in his house, John being seen near the scene of the burglary at the time when it was committed. He then suggests that these various clues, although they just *might* have other explanations, are not in general to be expected unless John had robbed the safe. Each clue is some evidence that he did rob the safe, confirms the hypothesis that John robbed the safe; and the evidence is cumulative – when put together it makes the hypothesis probable.

Let us call arguments of this kind arguments to a good explanation. Scientists use this pattern of argument to argue to the existence of unobservable entities as causes of the phenomena which they observe. For example, at the beginning of the nineteenth century, scientists observed many varied phenomena of chemical interaction, such as that substances combine in fixed ratios by weight to form new substances (e.g. hydrogen and oxygen always form water in a ratio by weight of 1:8). They then claimed that these phenomena would be expected if there existed a hundred or so different kinds of atom, particles far too small to be seen, which combined and recombined in certain simple ways. In their turn physicists postulated electrons, protons, and neutrons and other particles in order to account for the behaviour of the atoms, as well as for large-scale observable phenomena; and now postulate quarks in order to explain the behaviour of protons, neutrons and most other particles.

To be good arguments (that is, to provide evidence for their hypothesis), arguments of this kind must satisfy three criteria. First, the phenomena which they cite as evidence must not be very likely to occur in the normal course of things. We saw in the burglary example how the various clues, such as John's fingerprints on the safe, were not much to be expected in the normal course of things. Secondly, the phenomena must be much more to be expected if the hypothesis is true. If John did rob the safe it is *quite* likely that his fingerprints would be found on it. Thirdly, the hypothesis must be simple. That is, it must postulate the existence and operation of *few* entities, few *kinds* of entities, with few *easily* describable properties behaving in mathematically *simple* kinds of way. We could always postulate many new entities with complicated properties to explain anything which we find. But our hypothesis will only be supported by the evidence if it postulates few entities, which lead us to expect the diverse phenomena which form the evidence. Thus in the detective story example we could suggest that Brown planted John's fingerprints on the safe, Smith dressed up to look like John at the scene of the crime, and without any collusion with the others, Robinson hid the money in John's flat. This new hypothesis would lead us to expect the phenomena which we find just as well as does the hypothesis that John robbed the safe. But the latter hypothesis is confirmed by the evidence whereas the former is not. And this is because the hypothesis that John robbed the safe postulates *one* object – John – doing *one* deed – robbing the safe – which leads us to expect the several phenomena which we find. Scientists always postulate as few new entities (e.g. subatomic particles) as are needed to lead us to expect to find the phenomena which we observe; and they postulate that those entities do not behave erratically (behave one way one day, and a different way the next day) but that they behave in accordance with as simple and smooth a mathematical law as is compatible with what is observed. There is an old Latin saying, *simplex sigillum veri*, "The simple is the sign of the true". To be rendered probable by evidence, hypothesis must be simple.

The existence and order of the Universe

My first phenomenon which provides evidence for the existence of God is the existence of the universe for so long as it has existed (whether a finite time or, if it has no beginning, an infinite time). This is something evidently inexplicable by science. For a scientific explanation as such explains the occurrence of one state of affairs S_1 in terms of a previous state of affairs S_2 and some law of nature which makes states like S_2 bring about states like S_1. Thus it may explain the planets being in their present position by a previous state of the system (the Sun and planets being where they were last year) and the operation of Kepler's law which state that states like the latter are followed a year later by states like the former. *But what science by its very nature cannot explain is why there are any states of affairs at all.*

My next phenomenon is the operation of the most general laws of nature, that is, the orderliness of nature in conforming to very general laws. What exactly these laws are science may not yet have discovered – perhaps they are the field equations of Einstein's General Theory of Relativity, or perhaps there are some yet more fundamental laws. Now science can explain why one law operates in some narrow area, in terms of the operation of a wider law in the particular conditions of that narrow area. Thus it can explain why Galileo's law of fall holds – that small objects near the surface of the Earth fall with a constant acceleration towards the

Earth. Galileo's law follows from Newton's laws, given that the Earth is a massive body far from other massive bodies and the objects on its surface are close to it and small in mass in comparison. But what science by its very nature cannot explain is why there are the most general laws of nature that there are; for *ex hypothesi*, no wider law can explain their operation.

Scientific and personal explanation

That there is a Universe and that there are laws of nature are phenomena so general and pervasive that we tend to ignore them. But there might so easily not have been a universe at all, ever. Or the Universe might so easily have been a chaotic mess. That there is an *orderly* Universe is something very striking, yet beyond the capacity of science ever to explain. Science's inability to explain these things is not a temporary phenomenon, caused by the backwardness of twentieth century science. Rather, because of what a *scientific* explanation is, these things will ever be beyond its capacity to explain. For scientific explanations, by their very nature, terminate with some ultimate natural law and ultimate arrangements of physical things, and the questions which I am raising are why there are natural laws and physical things at all.

However, there is another kind of explanation of phenomena which we use all the time and which we see as a proper way of explaining phenomena. This is what I shall call *personal explanation*. We often explain some phenomenon E as brought about by a person P in order to achieve some purpose or goal G. The present motion of my hand is explained as brought about by me for the purpose of writing a philosophical paper. The cup being on the table is explained by a man having put it there for the purpose of drinking out of it. Yet this is a different way of explaining things from the scientific. Scientific explanation involves laws of nature and previous states of affairs. Personal explanation involves persons and purposes. If we cannot give a scientific explanation of the existence and orderliness of the Universe, perhaps we can give a personal explanation.

The Universe needs explaining

But why should we think that the existence and orderliness of the Universe has an explanation at all? We seek for an explanation of all things; but we have seen that we have only reason for supposing that we have found one if the purported explanation is simple, and leads us to expect what we find when that is otherwise not to be expected. The history of science shows that we judge that the complex, miscellaneous, coincidental and diverse needs explaining, and that it is to be explained in terms of something simpler. The motions of the planets (subject to Kepler's laws), the mechanical interactions of bodies on Earth, the behaviour of pendula, the motions of tides, the behaviour of comets, etc., formed a pretty miscellaneous set of phenomena. Newton's laws of motion constituted a simple theory which led us to expect these phenomena, and so was judged a true explanation of them. The existence of thousands of different chemical substances combining in different ratios to make other substances was complex. The hypothesis that there were only a hundred or so chemical elements of which the thousands of substances were made was a simple hypothesis which led us to expect the complex phenomenon.

Our Universe is a complex thing. There are lots and lots of separate chunks of it. The chunks have each a different finite and not very natural volume, shape, mass, etc. – consider the vast diversity of the galaxies, stars and planets, and pebbles on the sea shore. Matter is inert and has no powers which it can choose to exert; it does what it has to do. There is a limited amount of it in any region and it has a limited amount of energy and velocity. There is a complexity, particularity, and finitude about the Universe.

The conformity of objects throughout endless time and space to simple laws is likewise something which cries out for explanation. For let us consider what this amounts to. Laws are not things independent of material objects. To say that all objects conform to laws is simply to say that they all behave in exactly the same way. To say, for example, that the planets obey Kepler's laws is just to say that each planet at each moment of time has the property of moving in the ways that Kepler's laws state. There is therefore this vast coincidence in the behavioural properties of objects at all times and in all places. If all the coins of some region have the same markings, or all the papers in a room are written in the same handwriting, we seek an explanation in terms of a common source of these coincidences. We should seek a similar explanation of that vast coincidence which we describe as the conformity of objects to laws of nature – e.g. the fact that all electrons are produced, attract and repel other particles and combine with them in exactly the same way at each point of endless time and space.

God alone can explain it

The hypothesis of theism is that the Universe exists because there is a God who keeps it in being and that laws of nature operate because there is a God who brings it about that they do. He brings it about that the laws of nature operate by sustaining in every object in the universe its liability to behave in accord with those laws. He keeps the Universe in being by making the laws such as to conserve the matter of the Universe, i.e., by making it the case at each moment that what there was before continues to exist. The hypothesis is a hypothesis that a person brings about these things for some

7

purpose. He acts directly on the Universe, as we act directly on our brains, guiding them to move our limbs (but the Universe is not his body — for he could at any moment destroy it, and act on another universe, or do without a universe). As we have seen, personal explanation and scientific explanation are the two ways we have of explaining the occurrence of phenomena. Since there cannot be a scientific explanation of the existence of the Universe, either there is a personal explanation or there is no explanation at all. The hypothesis that there is a God is the hypothesis of the existence of the simplest kind of person which there could be. A person is a being with *power* to bring about effects, *knowledge* of how to do so, and *freedom* to make choices of which effects to bring about. God is by definition an omnipotent (that is, infinitely powerful), omniscient (that is, all knowing), and perfectly free person; he is a person of infinite power, knowledge, and freedom; a person to whose power, knowledge, and freedom there are no limits except those of logic. The hypothesis that there exists a being with infinite degrees of the qualities essential to a being of that kind is the postulation of a very simple being. The hypothesis that there is *such* a God is a much simpler hypothesis than the hypothesis that there is a god who has such and such a limited power. It is simpler in just the same way that the hypothesis that some particle has zero mass or infinite velocity, is simpler than the hypothesis that it has of 0.32147 of some unit or a velocity of 211,000 km/sec. A finite limitation cries out for an explanation of why there is just that particular limit, in a way that limitlessness does not.

That there should exist anything at all, let alone a universe as complex and as orderly as ours, is exceedingly strange. But if there is a God, it is not vastly unlikely that he should create such a universe. A universe such as ours is a thing of

8

beauty, and a theatre in which men and other creatures can grow and work out their destiny. The orderliness of the Universe makes it a beautiful Universe, but, even more importantly, it makes it a Universe which men can learn to control and change. For only if there are simple laws of nature can men predict what will follow from what – and unless they can do that, they can never change anything. Only if men know that by sowing certain seeds, weeding and watering them they will get corn, can they develop an agriculture. And men can only acquire that knowledge if there are easily graspable regularities of behaviour in nature. So God has good reason to make an orderly Universe and, *ex hypothesi*, being omnipotent, he has the power to do so. So the hypothesis that there is a God makes the existence of the Universe much more to be expected than it would otherwise be, and it is a very simple hypothesis. Hence the arguments from the existence of the Universe and its conformity to simple natural laws are good arguments to an explanation of the phenomena, and provide substantial evidence for the existence of God.

The Evolution of animals and man

The other phenomena which I have mentioned are also phenomena best explained by postulating the existence and creative activity of God, and so add to the cumulative case for his existence. Consider now the evolution of animals and humans. In the middle of the last century Darwin set out his impressive theory of evolution by natural selection to account for the existence of animals and humans. Animals varied in various ways from their parents (some were taller, some shorter, some fatter, some thinner, some had beginnings of a wing, others did not; and so on). Those animals with characteristics which made them best fitted to survive, survived and handed on their characteristics to the next generation. But, although in general resembling their parents, their offspring varied from them, and those variations which best fitted the animal to survive were again the ones most likely to be handed on to another generation. This process went on for millions of years producing the whole range of animals which we have today, each adapted to survive in a different environment. Among the characteristics giving advantage in the struggle for survival was intelligence, and the selections for this characteristic eventually led to the evolution of man. Such is Darwin's account of why we have today animals and men.

As far as it goes, his account is surely right. But there are two crucial matters beyond its scope. First, the evolutionary mechanism which Darwin describes works only because there are certains laws of biochemistry (animals produce many offspring, these vary in various ways from the parents, etc.) and certain features of the environment (there is a limited amount of food, drink, space, and so on). But why are there these laws rather than other laws? Perhaps because they follow from the most fundamental laws of physics. But the question then arises as to why the fundamental laws of physics are such as to give rise to laws of evolution. If we can answer this question we should do so. There is again available the same simpler answer – that there is a God who makes matter behave in accord with such laws in order to produce a world with animals and men. To develop my earlier point – a God has an obvious reason for producing men. He wants there to be creatures who can share in his creative work by making choices which affect the world they live in and the other creatures who live in that world. By the way we treat our environment and our bodies, bring up our children and influence our governments, we can make this world beautiful and its other inhabitants happy and knowledgeable; or we can make it ugly and its other inhabitants miserable and ignorant. A good God will seek other beings with whom to share in his activity of creation, of forming, moulding and changing the world. The fact of a mechanism to produce men is evidence of God behind that mechanism.

Secondly, Darwinian theory is concerned only with the physical characteristics of animals and men. Yet men have thoughts and feelings, beliefs and desires, and they make choices. These are events totally different from publicly observable physical events. Physical objects are, physicists tell us, interacting colourless centres of forces; but they act on our senses, which set up electrical circuits in our brains, and these brain events cause us to have sensations (of pain or colour, sound or smell), thoughts, desires and beliefs. Mental events such as these are no doubt largely caused by brain events (and vice-versa), but mental events are distinct from brain events – sensations are quite different from electro-chemical disturbances. They are in fact so different – private, coloured or noisy, and felt – from public events such as brain events, that it is very unlikely indeed that science will ever explain how brain events give rise to mental events (why this brain event causes a red sensation, and that one a blue sensation). Yet brain events do cause mental events; no doubt there are regular correlations between this type of brain events and that type of mental event, and yet no scientific theory can say why there are the particular correlations there are, or indeed any correlations at all (why did not evolution just throw up unfeeling robots?). Yet these correlations which science cannot explain cry out for explanation of another kind. That is available. God brings it about that brain events of certain kinds give

11

rise to mental events of certain kinds in order that animals and men may learn about the physical world, see it as embued with colour and smell making it beautiful, and learn to control it. Brain events caused by different sights, sounds and smells give rise to different and characteristic sensations and beliefs in order that men may have knowledge of a beautiful physical world and thus have power over it. Darwinianism can only explain why some animals are eliminated in the struggle for survival, not why there are animals and men at, all with mental lives of sensation and belief; and in so far as it can explain anything, the question inevitably arises why the laws of evolution are as they are. All this theism can explain.

Miracles
There are many reports of occasional miraculous events, events which violate laws of nature. Some of these reports are no doubt false, spead by unreliable witnesses. No doubt when men have claimed to see others levitate (float on air) or recover instantaneously from some disease, some of these reports are just false. Sometimes, too, when men have reported correctly some very strange event, although it seemed to be a violation of natural law, it was not. Magnetism might once have seemed miraculous to some people, but it is a perfectly orderly scientific phenomenon. But laying aside all such cases, there is a residue of apparently well-authenticated highly unusual events apparently contrary to laws of nature, but such as a God would have reason for bringing about (e.g. a spontaneous cure of cancer in answer to much prayer). Above all, there is the supreme reported miracle – the Resurrection of Jesus from the dead. This booklet cannot discuss the historical evidence for the Resurrection, but another booklet in this series *(Evidence for the*

Resurrection) will consider it in detail. In so far as that evidence is good evidence (as I believe it to be), it shows Jesus Christ to have been physically resurrected, an event which quite clearly violates the laws of nature and so calls for an explanation different from the scientific. That is available: God raised Christ from the dead to signify his acceptance of Christ's atoning sacrifice, to give his stamp of approval to his teaching, to take back Christ to Heaven where he belongs, and thereby to found a church to draw all men to himself.

Religious experience

Theism is able to explain the most general phenomena of science and, more particularly, historical facts, but it is also able to explain our own individual religious experiences. To so many men it has seemed at different moments of their lives that they were aware of God and his guidance. It is a basic principle of knowledge, which I have called the principle of credulity, that we ought to believe that things are as they seem to be, until we have evidence that we are mistaken. If it seems to me that I am seeing a table or hearing my friend's voice, I ought to believe this until evidence appears that I have been deceived. If you say the contrary – never trust appearances until it is proved that they are reliable – you will never have any beliefs at all. For what would show that appearances were reliable except more appearances? And if you can't trust appearances, you can't trust the further appearances either. Just as you must trust your five ordinary senses, so it is equally rational to trust your religious sense. An opponent may say, you trust your ordinary senses (e.g., your sense of sight) because it agrees with the senses of other men – what you claim to see they claim to see; but your religious sense does not argue with the senses of other men (they don't always have religious experiences at all, or of the same kind, as you do). However, it is important to realize that the rational man applies the principle of credulity before he knows what other men experience. You rightly trust your senses even if there is no other observer to check them. And if there is another observer who reports that he seems to see what you seem to see, you have thereafter to remember that he did so report, and that means relying on your own memory (again, how things seem) without present corroboration. Anyway, religious experiences often do coincide with those of many others in their general awareness of a power beyond ourselves guiding our lives. If some men do not have our experiences, even when our experiences coincide with those of others, that suggests that the former are blind to religious realities – just as a man's inability to see colours does not show that many of us who claim to see them are mistaken, only that he is colour blind. It is basic to human knowledge of the world that we believe things are as they seem to be in the absense of positive evidence to the contrary. Someone who seems to have an experience of God should believe that he does, unless evidence can be produced that he is mistaken. And it is another basic principle of knowledge that those who do not have an experience of a certain type ought to believe many others when they say that they do – again, in the absence of evidence of mass delusion.

Conclusion

The case for the existence of God is a cumulative one. I claim that the existence and continued operation of God (normally through the laws of nature, but sometimes setting them aside) can explain the whole pattern of science and history, and also men's most intimate religious experiences. The case for theism has to be balanced against any arguments against it (e.g. from the fact of evil and suffering in the world, which will be considered in another booklet in this series, *Evidence for the Love of God*). But in the absence of good contrary arguments, there is, I suggest, a strong case for the existence of God. As St Paul wrote in his *Epistle to the Romans* (1.20), 'the invisible things of God since the creation of the world are clearly seen, being perceived through the things that are made.'

This booklet is a very short and popular version of the full-scale and rigorous treatment of the issue contained in the author's *The Existence of God* (Clarendon Press, paperback).